TODAY'S MUSIC: GOOD OR BAD?

*A 4-week course to help (
teenagers understand an
contemporary music*

*by Stephen
Parolini*

Credits
Edited by Stephen Parolini
Cover designed by Jill Bendykowski and DeWain Stoll
Interior designed by Judy Atwood Bienick and Jan Aufdemberge
Illustrations by Corbin Hillam
Cover photo by David Priest and Brenda Rundback

ISBN 1-55945-101-7
Printed in the United States of America

CONTENTS

TODAY'S MUSIC: GOOD OR BAD?

"Tony!" his mom yelled, "Turn off that music and get to bed." Tony slumped in his chair with his homework untouched and headphones glued to his ears. Even if he could hear his mom calling, he probably wouldn't turn off the music. At least not for another three minutes and five seconds. His favorite song was playing.

● ● ●

"You gotta hear this," said Debra. "It's an awesome song." Debra's friends gathered around as she turned on the cassette player. Music blasted out of the speakers. Debra and her friends began to move to the beat.

"This is great!" said one friend.

"We'll have to play this at the dance!" said another.

● ● ●

Music.

Young people wouldn't know what to do without it. It filters into kids' lives every day. Radios. Cassette players. Concerts. Television. Movies. Some kids listen to escape, like Tony. Others enjoy the social benefits. Whatever the reason, music is everywhere. And junior highers listen to a lot of it.

So what's wrong with music? Nothing—unless it creates barriers between parents and kids, isolates kids from the real world, divides them into cliques or preaches messages that contradict Christian faith.

Music can do all those things. But it can also uplift people, bring friends closer together, praise God and challenge listeners to grow.

Today's Music: Good or Bad? will challenge your junior highers or middle schoolers to think critically about the music they listen to. It helps them communicate about their musical interests with parents. It shows kids how to be selective in what they listen to. And

34%
● Young people (ages 10 to 19) account for 34 percent of all recording sales in the United States.

60%
● Rock and pop music account for 60 percent of the music sales in the United States.

30%
● More than 30 percent of teenagers listen to at least 11 hours of recorded music each week.

it shows them how some music can actually help them grow as Christians.

Music is important to junior highers and middle schoolers. Acknowledge that. Then discover with them how it can be a positive part of their lives.

● Nearly 50 percent of teenagers listen to more than 11 hours of music on the radio each week.

● Eighty-eight percent of junior highers surveyed say they prefer doing their math with either the radio or television turned on.

HOW TO USE THIS COURSE

ACTIVE LEARNING

Think back on an important lesson you've learned in life. Did you learn it from reading about it? from hearing about it? from something you experienced? Chances are, the most important lessons you've learned came from something you experienced. That's what active learning is—learning by doing. And active learning is a key element in Group's Active Bible Curriculum.

Active learning leads students in doing things that help them understand important principles, messages and ideas. It's a discovery process that helps kids internalize what they learn.

Each lesson section in Group's Active Bible Curriculum plays an important part in active learning.

The **Opener** involves kids in the topic in fun and unusual ways.

The **Action and Reflection** includes an experience designed to evoke specific feelings in the students. This section also processes those feelings through "How did you feel?" questions and applies the message to situations kids face.

The **Bible Application** actively connects the topic with the Bible. It helps kids see how the Bible is relevant to the situations they face.

The **Commitment** helps students internalize the Bible's message and commit to make changes in their lives.

The **Closing** funnels the lesson's message into a time of creative reflection and prayer.

When you put all the sections together, you get a lesson that's fun to teach—and kids get messages they'll remember.

BEFORE THE 4-WEEK SESSION

● Read the Introduction, the Course Objectives and This Course at a Glance (p. 8).

● Decide how you'll publicize the course using the art on the Publicity Page (p. 9). Prepare fliers, newsletter articles and posters as needed.

● Look at the Bonus Ideas (p. 41) and decide which ones you'll use.

● Read the opening statements, Objectives and Bible Basis for the lesson. The Bible Basis shows how specific passages relate to junior highers and middle schoolers today.

● Choose which Opener and Closing options to use. Each is appropriate for a different kind of group. The first option is often more active.

● Gather necessary supplies from This Lesson at a Glance. Involve your kids in the class preparation. Have them take turns bringing portable stereo cassette players to class. Also ask kids to help you choose which tapes to use for the lessons that require music.

● Read each section of the lesson. Adjust where necessary for your class size and meeting room.

HELPFUL HINTS

● The approximate minutes listed give you an idea of how long each activity will take. Each lesson is designed to take 35 to 60 minutes. Shorten or lengthen activities to fit your group.

● If you see you're going to have extra time, do an activity or two from the "If You Still Have Time . . ." box or from the Bonus Ideas (p. 41).

● Dive into the activities with the students. Don't be a spectator. The lesson will be more successful and rewarding to both you and your students.

● As you discuss specific artists—both secular and Christian—be careful not to put them down. Concentrate on the artists' message rather than the artists' character.

● The answers given after discussion questions are responses your students *might* give. They aren't the only answers or the "right" answers. If needed, use them to spark discussion. Kids won't always say what you wish they'd say. That's why some of the responses given are negative or controversial. If someone responds negatively, don't be shocked. Accept the person and use the opportunity to explore other angles of the issue.

COURSE OBJECTIVES

By the end of this course your students will:
- understand why rock music is controversial;
- know how to listen selectively to music;
- understand how lyrics can affect their attitudes and feelings;
- learn to accept others regardless of the music they listen to;
- be thoughtful about and critical of lyrics; and
- be aware of Christian alternatives to non-Christian music.

THIS COURSE AT A GLANCE

Before you dive into the lessons, familiarize yourself with each lesson aim. Then read the scripture passages.
- Study them as a background to the lessons.
- Use them as a basis for your personal devotions.
- Think about how they relate to the music choices junior highers and middle schoolers make today.

LESSON 1: TURN OFF THAT NOISE!
Lesson Aim: To help kids understand why popular music is controversial and why parents are concerned about it.
Bible Basis: 1 Kings 12:5-16 and Proverbs 1:2-7.

LESSON 2: MESSAGES IN THE MUSIC
Lesson Aim: To help young people learn how to listen critically to music's messages.
Bible Basis: Romans 12:1-2 and Ephesians 5:6-17.

LESSON 3: STEREOTYPING
Lesson Aim: To help kids understand how to accept others even though they like different styles of music.
Bible Basis: Romans 14:1-12 and 1 Samuel 16:7.

LESSON 4: LISTENING ALTERNATIVES
Lesson Aim: To inform young people of Christian alternatives to harmful music and help them understand how music relates to their faith.
Bible Basis: Psalm 150 and Jude 20-21.

PUBLICITY PAGE

Grab your junior highers' attention! Copy this page, then cut and paste the art of your choice in your church bulletin or newsletter to advertise this course on today's music. Or copy and use the ready-made flier as a bulletin insert.

Splash this art on posters, fliers or even postcards! Just add the vital details: the date and time the course begins, and where you'll meet.

It's that simple.

A 4-week junior high course on the music kids listen to.

Come to _____

On_____

At _____

Discover how your faith relates to music!

TURN OFF THAT NOISE!

Today's popular music doesn't sound much like it did a few years ago. But some things don't change. Pop stars still sing about love. They're still in the public eye. And parents still misunderstand the music teenagers listen to.

To help kids understand why popular music is controversial and why parents are concerned about it.

Students will:
- talk about how parents respond to the music students like;
- discuss why they like the music they listen to;
- learn what the Bible says about seeking wisdom; and
- commit to talk with their parents about music.

Look up the following scriptures. Then read the background paragraphs to see how the passages relate to your junior highers or middle schoolers.

In **1 Kings 12:5-16,** young King Rehoboam follows the advice of his peers instead of the advice of Israel's elders.

As a new king, Rehoboam had to decide how to deal with the Israelites. So he sought the advice of the elders and his young peers. He ignored the advice of the elders, and his choice resulted in the splitting of the kingdom.

Like Rehoboam, young people must make difficult decisions—who to be friends with, what kind of music to listen to. Kids need to listen carefully to the advice of their elders—especially their parents. They don't always have to agree, but they do need to listen.

In **Proverbs 1:2-7**, Solomon urges readers to know wisdom and seek guidance.

Proverbs is for both the simple and the wise. And this

LESSON AIM

OBJECTIVES

BIBLE BASIS
1 KINGS 12:5-16
PROVERBS 1:2-7

passage reminds both that it's good to seek advice and knowledge in all areas of life.

Sometimes young teenagers think they don't need any help with decisions. But in all decisions, they should seek advice from parents and others who've "been there before." And parents should share their experience and wisdom with their sons and daughters.

THIS LESSON AT A GLANCE

Section	Minutes	What Students Will Do	Supplies
Opener (Option 1)	5 to 10	**What's That Noise?**—Listen to music they don't understand.	Cassette of foreign music, cassette player, paper, pencils
(Option 2)		**Parental Messages**—Discuss how parents feel about today's music.	Paper, pencils
Action and Reflection	10 to 15	**Why Rock?**—Discuss why they like the music they listen to.	Cassette and lyrics of a popular song, cassette player, paper, pencils
Bible Application	10 to 15	**Talking With the Elders**—Learn what the Bible says about seeking wisdom.	Bibles, paper, chocolate chip cookie recipe
Commitment	5 to 10	**Talking Music**—Commit to talk with their parents about the music they listen to.	"Talking Music" handouts (p. 17), pencils
Closing (Option 1)	5 to 10	**Adjusting the Volume**—Pray to be open with parents about the music they listen to.	Cassette from What's That Noise?, cassette player
(Option 2)		**New Messages**—Write prayers asking God to help them communicate with parents.	Paper from Parental Messages or blank paper, pencils

The Lesson

OPENER
(5 to 10 minutes)

OPTION 1: WHAT'S THAT NOISE?

As students arrive, have loud music in a foreign language playing. (Look for foreign music in your library.) Give kids each a piece of paper and a pencil. Have them write how the loud music makes them feel and what they think the music is saying. Turn off the music and have kids tell what they wrote. Then welcome them to the class and briefly introduce the topic for the next four weeks.

Ask:

● **How did the loud music make you feel?** (Uncomfortable; angry; it didn't bother me.)

● **How did you feel about not being able to understand the words?** (Confused; frustrated.)

● **How are your reactions to this music like the reactions your parents and other adults have to the music you listen to?** (Adults don't like the music I like either; adults can't understand the words.)

● **What are typical phrases your parents use when commenting on the music you listen to?** (Why do you listen to that music? Turn off that noise! I don't understand why you like that stuff.)

Say: **Parents don't always understand teenagers' music. Sometimes teenagers don't even understand it. Today, we'll look at ways you and your parents can talk about the music you like.**

OPTION 2: PARENTAL MESSAGES

Give each student a piece of paper and a pencil. Say: **On one side of your paper, list three things your parents might say about the music you listen to. On the other side, list three reasons you like the music.**

Form groups of no more than five.

Ask:

● **What are the most common responses parents have to your music?** (They don't like it; they just don't understand it.)

● **What are the most common reasons members of your group like their music?** (It sounds good; we like the beat; we like the words.)

● **Do you talk to your parents about the music you listen to? Why or why not?** (Yes, I like to keep them informed about what I like; no, it's none of their business; yes, they make me talk about it.)

Say: **Music is an important part of our lives. But sometimes it becomes a source of conflict for parents and teenagers. During this lesson, we'll focus on why music is controversial, and how you and your parents can turn this conflict area into a time of communication.**

WHY ROCK?

Form a circle. Introduce a popular song from the current Top 40 list found at most record stores. Then play the song. About halfway through the song, stop it and begin reading the rest of the lyrics in a dry, monotone voice.

Ask:

● **How did you feel when I stopped the music and**

ACTION AND REFLECTION
(10 to 15 minutes)

starting reading the song? (Angry; upset; confused; relieved.)

● **Did you prefer the song with the music or the spoken lyrics? Why?** (The music—you can't dance to lyrics; the spoken lyrics—I didn't like the music.)

Give each person a piece of paper and a pencil. Have students each list three songs they like. Then form pairs, and have partners each tell why they like the songs on their list—without speaking. Tell students they may draw pictures, mime actions or make noises, but they can't speak or write words to explain themselves.

Then ask:

● **How did you feel as you tried to describe why you liked the songs?** (Frustrated; embarrassed.)

● **How is this like trying to communicate with your parents about the music you like?** (I get frustrated, it's not easy to explain.)

● **How can knowing why you like the songs help you talk with your parents about the music you like?** (They'll understand better why I listen to it; it won't help; I can describe better why I like it.)

Say: **Music is an expression of your individuality. But when it creates conflict between you and your parents, music becomes a barrier.**

BIBLE APPLICATION
(10 to 15 minutes)

TALKING WITH THE ELDERS

Form a circle. Have someone read aloud 1 Kings 12:5-16. Ask:

● **What was King Rehoboam's problem?** (He was wondering how to deal with the Israelites.)

● **Whose advice did he seek?** (Elders' and peers'.)

● **What happened because he wouldn't listen to the elders?** (The kingdom split; the Israelites went home.)

● **When deciding what kind of music to listen to, whose advice do you follow—your friends' or parents'? Why?** (Friends'—they know me better; parents'—because I respect their opinions.)

● **If your parents complained about the music you were listening to, how would you respond?** (Ignore them; listen; explain why my music is okay.)

● **What might happen if you ignored their advice or refused to talk to them about your music?** (Nothing; our relationship would get worse; they'd be upset.)

Form groups no larger than four or five. Give each group a piece of paper and a pencil. Say: **You've just been told to fix chocolate chip cookies for a school project. But you can't find a recipe anywhere. As a group, come up with a recipe you think will work.**

Give groups a few minutes to come up with recipes. Then compare recipes with your sample recipe.

Ask:

● **How easy or difficult was this exercise?**

● **How would it have been different if someone who baked cookies often were in your group?**

Have someone read aloud Proverbs 1:2-7.

Ask:

● **What does it mean to "get guidance"?** (Talk with someone about something; ask for help with a problem.)

● **What kind of guidance could've improved your cookie recipe?** (A cookbook; have my mom in the group; someone who's baked cookies before.)

● **What kind of guidance can parents give regarding the music you listen to?** (They can help me think about the lyrics; they can't help much.)

● **How important is it to seek wisdom? Explain.** (Very important—we don't know all the answers so it helps to talk with others; not very important—I don't need anyone else's help.)

TALKING MUSIC

Give students each a "Talking Music" handout (p. 17). Have them complete the handout. Form pairs. Ask partners to talk about their completed handouts. Then say: **You probably didn't agree with everything your partner said or wrote. That's okay. Through openness and clear communication we can learn to accept each other and grow closer.**

Have kids each tell their partners one or two things they appreciated about them from their discussion of the handout.

Then distribute another copy of the handout to each student. Have kids each commit to take it home for their parent(s) to complete. Ask them to compare and discuss the completed handouts with their parents. Tell kids you'll talk about their discussions with parents during the next session.

OPTION 1: ADJUSTING THE VOLUME

Play the song loudly from the What's That Noise? opener. Say: **Parents often hear music just as you hear this song— they don't understand it. In order to get the most out of your music, you need to turn it off and talk about it with your parents.**

Turn off the music. During the silence, have students pray silently to be open with parents about the music they listen to.

Remind kids each to take home their "Talking Music" handouts and discuss them with their parents.

OPTION 2: NEW MESSAGES

Have students review their papers from Parental Messages,

COMMITMENT
(5 to 10 minutes)

CLOSING
(5 to 10 minutes)

or provide paper. Say: **Today we've discussed how important it is to talk with your parents about the music you listen to. On your paper write a short prayer. Ask God to help you be more open with parents about your musical interests. Also, ask God to help your parents be open to talking with you about your music.**

Remind kids each to take home their "Talking Music" handouts and discuss them with their parents.

If You Still Have Time . . .

Talking With Parents—Form groups of three or four. Have kids discuss times they've talked about music with their parents. Ask them to tell what went well in the conversation and what didn't.

A New Song (Part One)—Have kids each begin writing a song. Encourage them to write lyrics that express how they feel about music. Allow kids to work alone or with a friend to complete their songs over the next four weeks.

TALKING MUSIC

Conflict over music often comes from a lack of communication. Complete this handout and give a copy to your parent(s) to complete. Then discuss your responses together.

Rate each of the following factors according to their importance when deciding what kind of music to listen to or buy. Circle the appropriate number.

Factor	Not very important		Very important	
Image of the group/artist	1	2	3	4
Previous songs by the group/artist	1	2	3	4
Messages in the songs	1	2	3	4
Musical style	1	2	3	4
A friend's recommendation	1	2	3	4

Rank your favorite styles of music (1=favorite; 12=least favorite):

_____ Rock   _____ Dance Pop
_____ Rap   _____ Reggae
_____ Country   _____ Jazz
_____ Latin   _____ Soul
_____ Punk/New Wave   _____ Classical
_____ Heavy Metal   _____ Other (specify)_____

How do you feel when someone puts down the music you like?

What are positive aspects of the music you like?

What are negative aspects?

In 10 words or less, describe why you listen to your favorite music.

LESSON 2

MESSAGES IN THE MUSIC

Music is a means of communication. And today's music communicates many different messages. Junior highers and middle schoolers sometimes say they don't listen to the lyrics. But often, they sing along with their favorite songs. The lyrics do make an impact.

LESSON AIM

To help young people learn how to listen critically to music's messages.

OBJECTIVES

Students will:
- listen to popular songs and evaluate their messages;
- talk about how negative messages make them feel;
- learn what the Bible says about worldly messages; and
- commit to being selective in their music choices.

BIBLE BASIS

ROMANS 12:1-2
EPHESIANS 5:6-17

Look up the following scriptures. Then read the background paragraphs to see how the passages relate to your junior highers or middle schoolers.

In **Romans 12:1-2**, Paul urges readers not to conform to the world.

Paul encouraged members of the church in Rome to avoid living according to the lifestyle of the world. His message was simple: Set yourselves apart from those around you so you may be an example for others.

Music brings many messages into kids' lives. And lots of the messages go against the Christian lifestyle Paul encourages believers to live. Like the church in Rome, junior highers and middle schoolers must be careful not to conform to the ways of the world. And sometimes that means avoiding certain kinds of music.

In **Ephesians 5:6-17**, Paul warns readers to not be

deceived by empty words.

In Paul's time, there were lots of false prophets and teachings. In this passage, he describes how to avoid the deceptions of false teachings. He encourages believers to walk wisely and avoid empty words.

The empty words a junior higher hears come from many sources. Many of the songs they hear on the radio have little or no value. And others are outright deceptive. They promise success, love or meaning—but the promises are empty. Kids need to know how to discern the good messages from the deceptive ones.

THIS LESSON AT A GLANCE

Section	Minutes	What Students Will Do	Supplies
Opener (Option 1)	5 to 10	**Message Mania**—Look at record and tape jackets and guess the artists' messages.	Cassette or record jackets, tape, newsprint, markers
(Option 2)		**My Favorite Song**—Recall the lyrics in a song.	Paper, pencils
Action and Reflection	15 to 20	**Rate-a-Song**—Evaluate the messages in three popular songs.	"Rate-a-Song" handouts (p. 24), pencils, cassettes of three popular songs, cassette player, tape
Bible Application	5 to 10	**Listen Carefully**—Learn what the Bible says about negative messages.	Bibles, copies of Top 40 listings
Commitment	5 to 10	**Selectivity**—Commit to being selective in their music choices	"Pocket Message Detector" handouts (p. 24)
Closing (Option 1)	5 to 10	**Song Titles**—Write song titles that have positive messages.	3×5 cards, markers
(Option 2)		**Positive Thinking**—Think about how they feel when they hear positive messages.	Construction paper, pencils

The Lesson

OPTION 1: MESSAGE MANIA

Place cassette or record jackets around the room. Tape a sheet of newsprint next to each. Give students each a marker. Have them walk around the room and write on the appropriate newsprint what they think the music is about—based on the cover design. Then, for each cover, read the kids' comments.

Ask:

● **How similar were the responses?**

● **Why were there differences in the comments?** (We see things differently; you could read the cover different ways.) **similarities?** (The message of the cover was clear; some images are obvious.)

● **Can you judge the music just by looking at the cover? Why or why not?** (No—you don't have enough information; sometimes—the art can tell you a lot about the music.)

● **How much information do you need to judge the message of a song?** (You need to hear it; you need to read the words.)

Say: **Today we'll use as much information as possible to evaluate some popular songs. And we'll discuss how important it is to know what the songs are saying.**

OPTION 2: MY FAVORITE SONG

Give each person a piece of paper and a pencil. Ask kids each to think of a popular song they like. Give them a couple of minutes to write as many lyrics to the song as they can remember. Then have students trade papers with each other.

Say: **Look at the lyrics in front of you. Underline each phrase that's uplifting. Then circle each phrase that goes against Christian principles or is negative.**

Ask:

● **What did you find more of—good or bad phrases? Explain.**

● **What is the song trying to say?**

Say: **Lots of songs sound good. But many present negative or non-Christian messages. Today we'll look at the importance of the messages in the music we listen to.**

RATE-A-SONG

Tell kids you'll play three songs. Ask them to listen carefully to each song's lyrics. Give each student three copies of the "Rate-a-Song" handout (p. 24). Then have kids complete a handout for each song. Introduce and play a minute or two from each song, and give students time to complete the forms. Then tape the forms to the wall.

Have students walk around the room and read the "Rate-a-Song" handouts.

Then ask:
- **How do the ratings compare?**
- **How can a song's message be taken different ways?** (A song about love could really be about sex; some songs have double meanings.)
- **What's wrong with listening to songs with negative messages?** (Nothing; I don't know; they make you feel bad.)

Ask for two or three volunteers. Form a circle around them. Then tell the kids in the circle to call out negative messages to the volunteers. Suggest they say things such as: "Hate your neighbor"; "Drugs are cool"; "Don't make commitments to people"; "Life isn't worth living"; or "It doesn't matter if you're married."

After a minute or so, ask the volunteers:
- **How did you feel when you were given all the negative messages?** (It didn't bother me; I didn't like it.)
- **How easy is it to recall some of the messages?** (Very easy; difficult—I tried to ignore them.)
- **How is hearing these messages like listening to music with negative messages?** (It's no fun; I try to ignore those too.)

Ask kids to recall lyrics from any of the three songs they rated earlier. Then say: **When we listen to music, we hear the lyrics whether we want to or not. And some of those lyrics contain negative messages. Let's look at what the Bible has to say about negative messages.**

LISTEN CAREFULLY

Form groups of no more than five. Have them each read Romans 12:1-2 and Ephesians 5:6-17.

Ask:
- **What are "empty words"?** (Meaningless things; bad advice; negative words.)
- **What does Paul mean when he tells Christians not to conform to the world?** (Don't follow the lifestyle of non-Christians; don't be influenced by negative messages.)
- **How does Paul's advice apply to being selective in your music choices?** (We need to choose carefully what we listen to; we shouldn't be influenced by other people's interests.)

Give each group a copy of a Top 40 listing. Have the groups think about the songs on the list and circle those that contain empty words.

Then ask:
- **How many songs are nothing more than empty words? Explain.** (Many, a lot of songs don't have any meaning; some songs are silly, but most have something to say.)

BIBLE APPLICATION
(5 to 10 minutes)

● **Should you listen to songs that teach conformity to the world? Explain.** (Yes, if you just listen to the music it's okay; yes, the words don't hurt you; no, we should fill our minds with good stuff.)

● **How can you use the Bible's advice when you decide what to listen to?** (I can be careful about what I listen to; I can choose music that's positive instead of negative.)

● **How can you not conform to the world in your music choices?** (I can choose not to listen to popular music if it's bad; I can be selective in my choices.)

COMMITMENT
(5 to 10 minutes)

SELECTIVITY

Say: **Paul's advice is to be selective in what you listen to. But it's hard to tell sometimes what's good and what isn't.**

Distribute copies of the "Pocket Message Detector" (p. 24). Ask kids each to think of a popular song they like. Have them choose different songs from the ones used earlier. Have them follow the instructions on the card and see how the song rates. Form pairs to briefly discuss the results. Have partners commit to being selective in their music choices. Encourage them to use these cards to test the music they listen to.

Have kids share their experiences of talking with parents about the "Talking Music" handout (p. 17) from the previous session.

Ask:

● **How did your parents respond when you told them you wanted to talk about music?** (They were surprised; they didn't have time; they were open to it.)

● **How did you feel after talking with your parents? Why?** (Relieved—they were glad to talk; uncomfortable—they didn't understand why I wanted to talk with them; angry—they didn't listen to me.)

● **How can your parents help you be selective in your choice of music?**

Table Talk

The Table Talk activity in this course helps junior highers and middle schoolers discuss music choices and issues with their parents.

If you choose to use the Table Talk activity here, show students the "Table Talk" handout (p. 25). Ask them to spend time with their parents completing it. Before kids leave, give them each the "Table Talk" handout to take home or tell them you'll be sending it to their parents.

Or use the Table Talk idea found in the Bonus Ideas (p. 42) for a meeting based on the handout.

OPTION 1: SONG TITLES

Give each student a 3×5 card and marker. Have them each make up five "song titles" that express positive feelings and love for God and write them on their card. Say: **God has given us the ability and desire to enjoy music. Yet we need to choose carefully what we listen to.**

Have kids each read aloud one or two of their song titles.

Then have kids each write on the back of the card one specific thing they appreciate about other class members. Remind them this is a time to be sincere and serious. Then have kids form a circle and pass the cards around for everyone to read.

Close by singing a familiar chorus.

OPTION 2: POSITIVE THINKING

Say: **Although there are many negative messages in popular music today, there are also some positive ones.**

Give kids each a piece of construction paper. Have them each tell about a song they like that has a positive message. Then have them each tear their paper into a shape that represents how they feel when they hear a song with an uplifting or positive message. Have kids each write their name on their paper.

Have students place the shapes on a table. Have kids go around and write one or two positive words on each person's paper shape. Encourage kids to be sincere. Then have kids each pick up and read their paper. Form a circle around the table and close with prayer, thanking God for the songs with positive messages.

CLOSING
(5 to 10 minutes)

If You Still Have Time . . .

Musical Message Chairs—Preview popular songs to find one that has negative messages. Play a variation of musical chairs. Instead of having kids sit down when the music stops, have them sit whenever they hear a negative message in the song. After kids sit down, briefly discuss what was negative about the message.

A New Song (Part Two)—Give students time to continue writing their songs from the first lesson (p. 16).

RATE A SONG

Rate the following characteristics from 1 to 10.

Name of song: _____

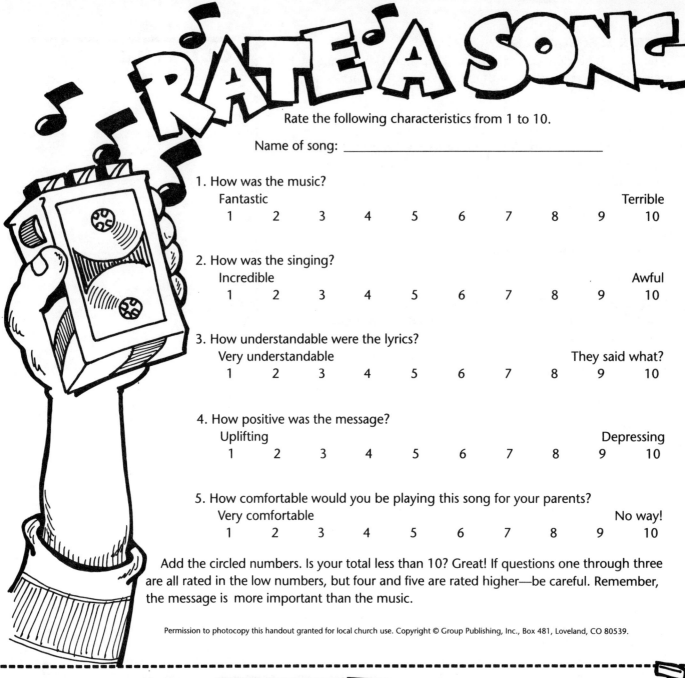

1. How was the music?
Fantastic   Terrible

1   2   3   4   5   6   7   8   9   10

2. How was the singing?
Incredible   Awful

1   2   3   4   5   6   7   8   9   10

3. How understandable were the lyrics?
Very understandable   They said what?

1   2   3   4   5   6   7   8   9   10

4. How positive was the message?
Uplifting   Depressing

1   2   3   4   5   6   7   8   9   10

5. How comfortable would you be playing this song for your parents?
Very comfortable   No way!

1   2   3   4   5   6   7   8   9   10

Add the circled numbers. Is your total less than 10? Great! If questions one through three are all rated in the low numbers, but four and five are rated higher—be careful. Remember, the message is more important than the music.

- -

POCKET MESSAGE DETECTOR

Answer the following questions about the song you're testing.

- Does it make you feel bad or depressed after hearing it?
- Does it make fun of a group of people?
- Does it equate love with sex?
- Does it use violent images?
- Does the message go against your Christian faith?
- Would you be uncomfortable singing this song for your parents? for Jesus?

Check your answers. If you answered "yes" a bunch—watch out. The song may not be worth listening to. Talk with your parents and Christian friends about it. Then decide.

Table Talk

To the Parent: We're talking about contemporary music at church. Please sit down with your junior higher or middle schooler and talk about this subject. Use this sheet to spark discussion.

Parent

Tell your junior higher:
- about a song that makes you happy.
- about a song that makes you depressed.
- why songs can affect your feelings.
- what kind of music you listened to when you were a teenager.
- how your parents responded to the music you listened to.

Junior higher

Tell your parent:
- about a song that makes you happy.
- about a song that makes you depressed.
- why songs can affect your feelings.

Parent and junior higher

Each of you collect three or four of your favorite albums. Pick one song on each, play it and explain why you like it. Then answer the following questions for each song:
- What style of music is this song?
- What's the song trying to say?
- How are the lyrics positive or negative?
- How do the lyrics challenge the listener?

MUSICAL COVENANT

Read and complete the following covenant. Then, after agreeing on its content, sign and date it. Work together to stay within the guidelines of the covenant.

Music is an important part of our lives. We know it sometimes becomes a barrier in our relationship. With this covenant, we agree to talk about any concerns we have about the music we listen to.

I, _____ (teenager), promise to keep the volume down on my stereo and have _____ minutes/hours of quiet time each day for studying, reading or other activity. I'll be open to talking about music conflicts we may have.

I, _____ (parent), promise to be honest about my concerns but also willing to negotiate when a conflict occurs. I will also follow the same guidelines I set for my teenager for volume level of music and quiet time.

We promise to be selective in our choices of music.

Signed _____ Date _____

Signed _____ Date _____

Signed _____ Date _____

LESSON 3

STEREOTYPING

Punkers. Headbangers. Rappers. New wavers.

Junior highers and middle schoolers often categorize each other based on the music they listen to. And sometimes those categories become barriers.

LESSON AIM

To help kids understand how to accept others even though they listen to different styles of music.

OBJECTIVES

Students will:
● examine how it feels to be stereotyped;
● learn the importance of looking beyond a person's appearance;
● learn how musical choices can be "statements"; and
● look at what the Bible says about judging others.

BIBLE BASIS
ROMANS 14:1-12
1 SAMUEL 16:7

Look up the following scriptures. Then read the background paragraphs to see how the passages relate to your junior highers or middle schoolers.

In **Romans 14:1-12**, Paul warns readers not to judge one another.

In this passage, Paul describes attitudes Christians should have toward one another in "gray" areas of life. He tells Christians to respect each other regardless of the strength of their faith.

When a junior higher sees peers dressed in full heavy metal regalia and listening to the latest heavy metal band, it's easy to make quick—and often inaccurate—judgments about those peers. Although Paul speaks primarily about judging people's faith, his message applies to kids who judge each other based on other things such as music, appearance and activities.

In **1 Samuel 16:7**, God tells Samuel not to look at the outward appearance of man.

Samuel was quick to single out the son who appeared most capable and assume the Lord meant to have Eliab as the new king. That's when the Lord reminded Samuel that God looked at the heart, not the outward appearance. David, the youngest son, was chosen instead.

There are two messages for junior highers in this passage. First, they can learn the lesson Samuel learned: It isn't right to judge someone based on outward appearance. And second, kids can be assured that no matter how inadequate or weak they might feel—God is more concerned about their hearts.

THIS LESSON AT A GLANCE

Section	Minutes	What Students Will Do	Supplies
Opener (Option 1) (Option 2)	5 to 10	**Different Tastes**—Form groups based on their interests. **Similar Interests**—Discuss things they have in common with friends.	Doughnuts, plates, marker, paper Paper, pencils
Action and Reflection	10 to 15	**Musical Descriptions**—Define traits of specific groups and discuss the problems of stereotyping.	Newsprint, tape, markers, "Musical Descriptions" handout (p. 32), pencils
Bible Application	10 to 15	**Inside and Out**—Learn what the Bible says about judging people.	Bibles, construction paper, pencils
Commitment	5 to 10	**New Music**—Listen to a variety of musical styles and discuss what's most important in evaluating a song.	Cassettes of different music styles, cassette player, "Musical Descriptions" handout
Closing (Option 1) (Option 2)	5 to 10	**Hearts of Acceptance**—Create a symbol of their acceptance of people who're different. **Song and A Prayer**—Write prayers, and then read them as they hum a familiar chorus.	"Musical Descriptions" handout, paper from Inside and Out Paper, pencils

The Lesson

OPTION 1: DIFFERENT TASTES

Bring enough doughnuts for all students. Include four different kinds. Place each kind of doughnut on a separate plate and place each plate in a different location. Number the locations one to four. For example, all cake doughnuts might be at location one, all glazed doughnuts at location two, and so on.

Have students walk around the room and look at the dif-

O P E N E R
(5 to 10 minutes)

ferent kinds of doughnuts. Then have them stand next to the kind they like best.

Say: **We often judge others based on what they wear, do, listen to or eat. And sometimes, we base friendships on the same things. You now stand with people who like the same kind of doughnuts. This is your Doughnut Group. But don't eat the doughnuts yet. I'm going to list some activities and interests you may have. For each, I'll direct you to stand near one of the doughnut stations. After I read the options, you may each move to the appropriate station.**

Pause between each question. Kids will probably move several times.

Which sport do you like best?
 If baseball, move to station one.
 If football, move to station two.
 If tennis, move to station three.
 If you don't like sports much, move to station four.
Which school subject do you like best?
 If math, move to station one.
 If English, move to station two.
 If science, move to station three.
 If art, move to station four.
Which kind of movies do you like best?
 If mysteries or thrillers, move to station one.
 If comedies, move to station two.
 If dramas, move to station three.
 If adventures, move to station four.
Which musical style do you like best?
 If heavy metal, move to station one.
 If pop/rock, move to station two.
 If new wave or punk, move to station three.
 If country, move to station four.

Tell students they may have a doughnut from the station they ended up next to. Then have them sit down.

Ask:

● **How many people outside your original doughnut group did you have other things in common with?** (Lots; a few; none.)

Say: **Imagine how many friendships you might miss out on if you based your friendships solely on one thing—such as what kind of doughnut you like. Or your favorite music. Today we'll look at ways to break down stereotypes and learn to accept others no matter what their interests.**

OPTION 2: SIMILAR INTERESTS

Give each student a piece of paper and a pencil. Have them each list the names of three friends. Then have them list things they have in common with each friend next to the appropriate name. Have kids each turn their paper over and write the names again. This time, have them list things they don't have in common with each friend.

Afterward, ask:

● **Which were easier to think of—common things or differences? Explain.**

● **If you could only associate with people who like almost everything you like, how long would your list of friends be?** (The same; very short.)

● **How would you feel if you only had friends who were just like you?** (I wouldn't like it; it wouldn't bother me.)

● **Why is it important to have friends who don't like the same things you do?** (They help you grow; they suggest new ideas; it's good to disagree.)

Say: **When we choose friends, we often look for people who like the same things we do. The same movies, the same teachers, the same music. But that can exclude people. Today, we'll look at how we can avoid stereotyping people based on the music they listen to.**

MUSICAL DESCRIPTIONS

Say: **What mental picture do you get when you hear the words "heavy metal"?** (Pause) **"soul"?** (Pause) **"country and western"?**

Pause for a moment.

Say: **If you're like most people, you probably pictured a person wearing a type of clothing you associate with each musical style.**

Tape eight sheets of newsprint to the wall. On each sheet draw a large stick figure. At the top of each sheet, write one of the following musical styles: punk/new wave, heavy metal, dance, country, rock, rap, new age and soul.

Have students walk around and draw things they attribute to each musical style next to the appropriate stick figure. Have them draw appropriate clothing and paraphernalia on the stick figures.

Distribute the "Musical Descriptions" handouts (p. 32) and pencils. Ask students each to complete their handout. Have junior highers tell which words they attributed to each musical style on the "Musical Descriptions" handout.

Ask:

● **How accurate are these descriptions and pictures?**

● **Look at the style of music you like best. Do you fit these traits? How does the list make you feel?** (No, angry; no, it doesn't bother me; yes, pleased; yes, surprised.)

● **How are these lists like stereotypes?** (They lump everyone into the same group; they don't allow for individuality.)

● **What's wrong with stereotyping?** (Nothing; it isn't fair.)

● **How do you feel when someone avoids you because of the people you hang around with?** (Angry; it doesn't bother me.)

ACTION AND REFLECTION
(10 to 15 minutes)

BIBLE APPLICATION
(10 to 15 minutes)

INSIDE AND OUT

Read aloud Romans 14:1-12.

Ask:

● **What does the passage say about judging others?** (We shouldn't judge people.)

● **How is judging people like stereotyping?** (You're saying something about someone you don't know.)

● **How do you feel when someone misjudges you?** (Angry; upset; it doesn't bother me.)

Read aloud 1 Samuel 16:7. Say: **It's easy for us to judge people by their dress or music. According to this passage, God is more interested in what's on the inside.**

Give students each a piece of light-color construction paper and a pencil. In the center of their paper, have them each write how God judges people.

Ask:

● **Does outward appearance matter at all? Why or why not?** (No, because it's what you believe that counts; yes, it reflects how you feel inside.)

● **Do people make statements by the kind of music they listen to? Explain.** (Yes, if they want to look tough they listen to heavy metal; no, people just choose what they like.)

● **What does the music you listen to say about you?**

COMMITMENT
(5 to 10 minutes)

NEW MUSIC

Play a minute or less from songs representing a variety of musical styles, such as heavy metal, country, jazz, pop, soul, Latin or new wave. Then have students look around at the way they're dressed.

Say: **A musical style can be like the clothing we choose to wear. Sometimes it makes a statement, but mostly it serves as packaging for something more important. Different music styles are like different fashions. You may like one and hate another. And just as we can't judge people based on how they look, we can't judge songs based solely on the music style. The best way to know the value of a song is to hear its message. And the best way to know a person better is to understand his or her beliefs.**

Form pairs. Have partners each say two or three things they appreciate about their partner. Remind students this is a time to be serious and not to goof off.

Have students each write a prayer of commitment in the box at the bottom of the "Musical Descriptions" handout. Encourage them to commit to looking beyond people's outward appearance.

Table Talk Follow-Up

If you sent the "Table Talk" handout (p. 25) to parents last week, discuss students' reactions to the activity. Ask volunteers to share what they learned from the discussion with their parents.

OPTION 1: HEARTS OF ACCEPTANCE

Form a circle. Have students each follow the dotted lines and tear out the inside of their "Musical Descriptions" handout. Ask them each to place this handout on top of the construction paper from the Inside and Out activity. Say: **When we tear away the stereotypes we can see the heart. Read inside the heart to see how you should see others.**

Close in prayer, asking God to help us get beyond the packaging to the real person and the real meaning.

OPTION 2: SONG AND A PRAYER

Have students each write a one-sentence prayer, asking God to help them look beyond outward appearances.

Form a circle. Then have kids sing one or two verses of a familiar chorus. Have them then hum the chorus as they pass around and silently read their prayers.

CLOSING
(5 to 10 minutes)

If You Still Have Time . . .

Breaking Down the Walls—Form groups of no more than five. Give each group a supply of newspapers and tape. Have them each build a wall around their group. Then say: **Judging people based on the music they listen to is like building a wall around yourself. You limit yourself to accepting only those people who're like you. With God's help we can break down the barriers and get to know people on the inside.**

Have kids break out of their walls and go around the room shaking hands with each other.

A New Song (Part Three)—Give students time to finish writing their songs from the first and second weeks (p. 16 and 23).

MUSICAL DESCRIPTIONS

How would you describe people who like certain styles of music? Draw lines connecting descriptive words in the center of the heart with the musical style or styles they best fit.

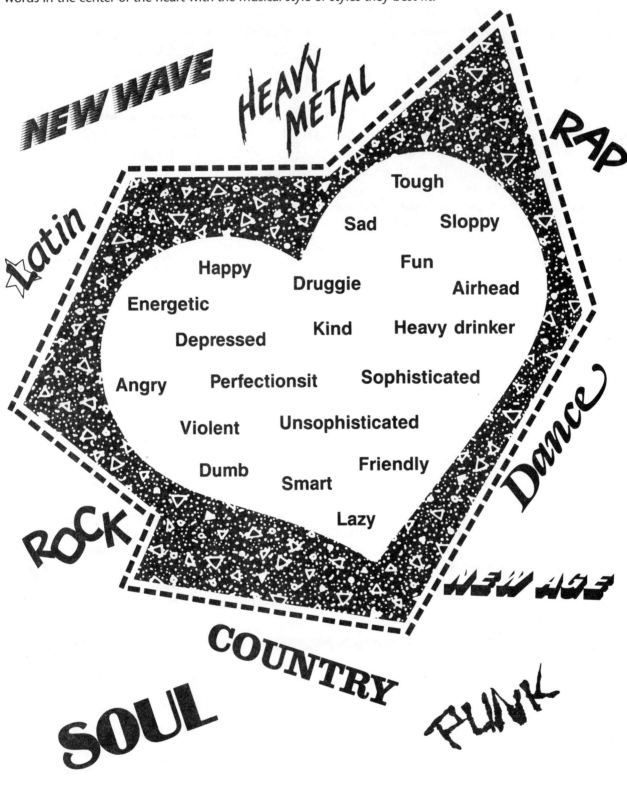

LISTENING ALTERNATIVES

T he messages in many secular songs go against the Christian lifestyle. Today, there's an alternative to the negative songs. Christian music now comes in just about every possible musical style. But just because it's Christian, does that mean it's good?

LESSON AIM

To inform young people of Christian alternatives to harmful music and help them understand how music relates to their faith.

OBJECTIVES

Students will:
- discuss what makes something "Christian";
- learn about the Christian alternative to negative music;
- examine what the Bible says about the purpose of music; and
- learn how to make good decisions about the music they listen to.

BIBLE BASIS

PSALM 150
JUDE 20-21

Look up the following scriptures. Then read the background paragraphs to see how the passages relate to your junior highers or middle schoolers.

In **Psalm 150**, the Psalmist sings praises to the Lord.
Music played an important role in the Old Testament times. And the book of Psalms was the hymnal of the Jewish people. Many of the Psalms, such as Psalm 150, are songs of praise and thanksgiving to God.
Christian music has changed greatly over the years. Hymnals now contain not only the classical hymns, but also popular contemporary choruses. Junior highers can now listen to the Psalmist's message to the beat of a drum and sound of an electric guitar. The music may have changed, but the mes-

sage of praise is the same.

In **Jude 20-21**, Jude encourages readers to build themselves up in faith.

This letter is directed to a group of believers who'd gotten involved in all kinds of lawlessness. Jude's message was: "Contend for the faith."

Some of today's popular music teaches the same kind of falsehoods the early church had to deal with. But following Jude's advice, junior highers can choose music that challenges them to build their faith. Much Christian music—and some secular music—can do just that.

THIS LESSON AT A GLANCE

Section	Minutes	What Students Will Do	Supplies
Opener (Option 1)	up to 5	**Good Taste?**—Decide which kind of food tastes best.	Carrots, candy bars
(Option 2)		**Positive Messages**—Rewrite the lyrics of a popular song to make it "Christian."	Popular song lyrics, paper, pencils
Action and Reflection	10 to 15	**Christian vs. Non-Christian?**—Discuss the differences between secular and Christian songs	"Christian vs. Non-Christian" handouts (p. 39), pencils
Bible Application	15 to 20	**Growth and Praise**—Look at two ways contemporary Christian music can help Christians grow.	Bibles, newsprint, markers, tape, music cassettes, cassette player
Commitment	5 to 10	**Now Hear This**—Commit to listening to music that praises God or challenges their faith to grow.	"Commitment Disc" handouts, (p. 40), pencils, music cassettes, cassette player
Closing (Option 1)	5 to 10	**Musical Celebration**—Celebrate their enjoyment of music.	Balloons, streamers, confetti, music cassettes, cassette player
(Option 2)		**Musical Prayer**—Listen to a contemporary Christian song as a closing prayer.	Music cassette, cassette player

The Lesson

OPENER
(up to 5 minutes)

OPTION 1: GOOD TASTE?

Place carrots and candy bars on a table. Have students each pick one item, but not eat it yet. Have them look around at what each person picked.

Then ask:

● **Which items were more popular—carrots or candy bars? Why?**

Have kids share the candy bars and each take a bite of one of the carrots.

Ask:

● **Which item tastes better to you?**

● **Which item is better for you?**

Say: **Imagine someone just invented a great-tasting candy bar that contained all the nutrients of a carrot and none of the sugar or caffeine of a candy bar.**

Ask:

● **If you could choose the carrot, a real candy bar or the new candy bar, which would you choose? Why?** (The new candy bar—because you get the flavor without the bad side effects; the original candy bar—because I don't trust new ideas; the carrot—because I know it's good for me.)

Say: **Contemporary Christian music is like that new candy bar. It has all the excitement and taste of popular music, but usually contains nutrients that help your faith grow healthy instead of giving you a spiritual stomachache.**

OPTION 2: POSITIVE MESSAGES

Form groups of three or four. Give groups each a copy of lyrics from a popular secular song (popular songs about love work best), a piece of paper and a pencil. Have groups read the lyrics and cross out any words or phrases that go against Christian beliefs. Then have groups share their edited versions with the other groups. Have students discuss whether they agree or disagree that the items should be edited out.

Ask:

● **How much of the song did you have to edit?**

● **Were you surprised at how many of the lyrics were non-Christian? Why or why not?** (Yes, I didn't think they were that bad; no, I don't think they're non-Christian anyway.)

● **How might this song affect you?** (It might make me feel depressed; it could influence how I act.)

● **Would this song appeal to you more or less if it had lyrics that challenged your faith in a positive way? Explain.** (More, I'd enjoy the positive message; less, I like the song the way it is; neither, I don't listen to the words.)

Say: **We can't change the lyrics in popular songs. But we can choose wisely what songs we listen to. With contemporary Christian music, you can hear positive lyrics in the musical styles you like best.**

CHRISTIAN VS. NON-CHRISTIAN?

Form a circle.

Ask:

● **What's the first thing you think of when you hear the phrase Christian music?** (Amy Grant; boring; hymns; Petra.)

Say: **Christian music is as varied as popular music. There are Christian rappers, rock bands and even instrumental artists.**

Ask:

● **But just because music is called Christian, does that make it good? Why or why not?** (No; it may be poorly done; no, the message may be trite; yes, it's always better than non-Christian stuff.)

Form groups of four or five. Give each group a copy of the "Christian vs. Non-Christian" handout (p. 39). Assign each group a different topic from the following list:

● sex   ● drugs   ● money   ● love   ● happiness

Have groups each complete their handout using their assigned topic. Then have them each share their completed handout with the other groups.

Ask:

● **What are differences between the Christian approach to a topic and the non-Christian approach?** (Christian approach is positive; non-Christian approach is sometimes negative or harmful.)

● **What are similarities?** (Both reflect beliefs; both try to influence people.)

● **What are some popular songs with messages that don't go against Christianity?**

● **How can you learn from both Christian and non-Christian messages?** (Non-Christian messages can challenge me to think about an issue; Christian messages can uplift or challenge my faith.)

GROWTH AND PRAISE

Have a young person read aloud Psalm 150.

Then ask:

● **According to this Psalm, how should we praise God?** (With music; with instruments; with singing.)

● **Why is it important to praise God?** (It's part of our worship; it makes us feel good; it makes God feel good.)

Say: **Music that praises God has been around for many years. In Old Testament times, the Psalms were sung much as we sing hymns today. To this day, some denominations still use the Psalms as hymns. But now all kinds of contemporary music can praise God.**

Form groups of three or four. Give each group a sheet of newsprint and some markers. Have groups each design a poster that praises God. While they design the posters, play contemporary Christian praise songs. Check a Christian bookstore for the latest songs or use classics such as:

"Awesome God" by Rich Mullins; "Great is the Lord" by Michael W. Smith or "Sing Your Praise to the Lord" by Amy Grant. Tape the posters to the wall.

Have a young person read aloud Jude 20-21.

Ask:

● **What are ways we build our faith?** (Reading the Bible; praying; going to church.)

Say: **Even the music we listen to can challenge us to grow as Christians. Much of contemporary Christian music deals with everyday struggles and challenges us to grow in faith.**

Play a portion of a song that challenges Christians to grow. Check out the bookstore or use older songs such as: "Bye Bye Babylon" by Whiteheart (about pride); "Someone To Hold On To" by The Choir (about leaning on God's strength); or "Young Boy Young Girl" by Rick Cua (about waiting until marriage for sex).

Then ask:

● **What was the song about?**

● **How does this song challenge your faith?**

Say: **Contemporary Christian music can be worshipful. And it can challenge you to think about your relationship with God. Both Christian rock—and some popular music— can challenge you to think about issues you may deal with daily, such as peer pressure, drugs and alcohol, dating, sex and sharing your faith.**

NOW HEAR THIS

Give each student a copy of the "Commitment Disc" handout (p. 40). Have kids complete it. Play a contemporary Christian song in the background as they work. Form pairs. Have partners briefly discuss the handout. Then have them encourage each other to begin listening to songs that challenge or uplift them.

OPTION 1: MUSICAL CELEBRATION

Form groups of three or four. Give groups each a supply of balloons, streamers and confetti.

Say: **Uplifting music is like a celebration. Each time we hear people sing of their love for God, we can rejoice with them.**

Have groups each decorate an area of the room with the streamers and balloons. Play an energetic song during the decorating. Use a new song or one of the following older songs: "Lead Me On" by Amy Grant; "Keep the Fire Burning" by Stryper; "On Fire" by Petra; "Don't Stop the Music" by DeGarmo and Key.

After the song ends, close with a short prayer, thanking God for music and the ability to enjoy it and be challenged by it. Thank each student for his or her contributions to the

COMMITMENT
(5 to 10 minutes)

CLOSING
(5 to 10 minutes)

class. Be specific. Then have kids all toss the confetti as the prayer's "amen."

OPTION 2: MUSICAL PRAYER
Have a time of silent prayer as you play a contemporary Christian song. Use a new song or one of the following: "Oh Lord, You're Beautiful" by Keith Green (or a newer version by Kim Boyce); "Psalm 1" by Kim Hill; or "Saved by Love" by Amy Grant.

Following the silent prayer, thank each student for his or her contribution to the class. Be specific.

If You Still Have Time ...

Course Reflection—Form a circle. Ask students to reflect on the past four lessons. Have them take turns completing the following sentences:
- Something I learned in this course was . . .
- If I could tell my friends about this course, I'd say . . .
- Something I'll do differently because of this course is . . .

A New Song (Part Four)—Have kids share their completed songs with the rest of the group. Encourage them to continue to write songs and poems for personal devotions and sharing with friends.

CHRISTIAN VS. NON-CHRISTIAN

As a group, complete the following handout. In the left column, write answers a Christian songwriter might give. In the right column, write answers a non-Christian songwriter might give.

Your topic: _____

Christian Response   **Non-Christian Response**

1. What would you say about
this topic in a song?

2. What would motivate you to
write this song?

3. What would the album cover
for the song look like?

4. How would you want the song
to affect people?

5. Would the song reflect your
beliefs? Why or why not?

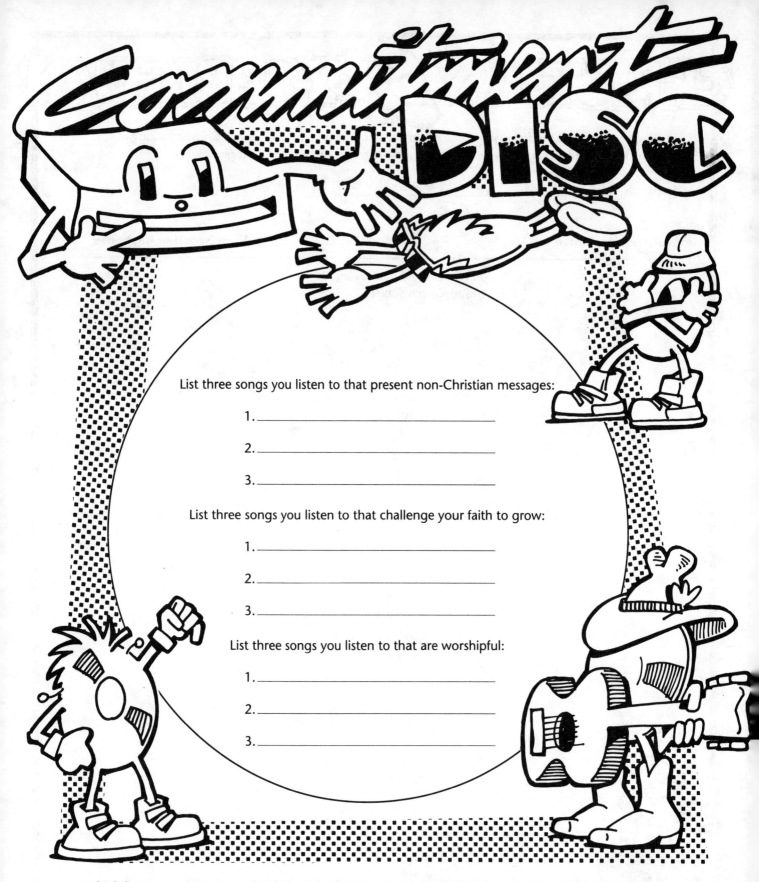

Commitment DISC

List three songs you listen to that present non-Christian messages:

1. _____
2. _____
3. _____

List three songs you listen to that challenge your faith to grow:

1. _____
2. _____
3. _____

List three songs you listen to that are worshipful:

1. _____
2. _____
3. _____

Which list was easier to complete? If you had a hard time completing the second and third lists, seek out music that builds your faith and praises God. Check out the latest contemporary Christian music in your favorite style at a Christian bookstore. Choose three songs with positive or challenging messages. Then stop listening to the three songs you listed for the first question and listen to the Christian songs instead. Begin changing your listening habits to include only songs that challenge you to grow or help you worship.

BONUS IDEAS

Old and New—Invite parents to bring their favorite records and tapes from their junior high years to a meeting with the students. Have junior highers bring their favorite current hits. Form mixed groups of parents and kids and have them listen to old and new music. Have the groups discuss the messages in the music. For a fun twist, have parents and kids each present a lip-sync to one of their favorite songs.

Intergenerational Worship Service—Have kids put together a worship service that uses a variety of music styles. Have kids use 1 Corinthians 12 as a basis for the message portion of the service. Encourage them to include both adults and young people in the service and sing songs representing everyone's favorite musical styles.

Comparison Chart—Order a copy of the "Music Comparison Chart." This chart lists and matches about 200 contemporary Christian artists and groups with similar-sounding secular artists and groups. Contact Music Helps at Box 118165, Carrollton, TX 75011.

Ministry Support—Have junior highers or middle schoolers write letters of encouragement to their favorite Christian artist. Many cassette album or compact disc jackets list addresses for corresponding with the artists. Or letters can be addressed in care of the artist's record company.

Concert Time—Find local Christian artists. Then help your students plan a concert featuring some of these artists. Work with the kids to choose the best groups. Invite members of other junior high or middle school youth groups and Sunday school classes.

Christian Music Investigation—Arrange with a Christian bookstore to give your students a "tour" of Christian music. Take kids to the store and have a bookstore employee play portions of cassettes by popular Christian artists. Then encourage them to consider a Christian artist the next time they plan to buy music.

Music Resources—Keep up with the latest developments in contemporary Christian music—and help your students keep up—by subscribing to Contemporary Christian Magazine (CCM). Contact CCM, Box 6300, Laguna Hills, CA 92654.

Or order "Top Music Countdown," a quarterly booklet and pull-out poster that examines popular music from a Christian perspective. Don Kimball's Cornerstone Media also has audio cassettes available on a wide variety of topics. One tape, "Dirty Dozen," analyzes 12 popular songs that promote negative values. Another, "Psalm 151," takes a look at popular songs that promote positive values.

Contact Cornerstone Media, Box 6236, Santa Rosa, CA 95406 for more information.

For another perspective on music, check out "Media Update," a bimonthly publication from Menconi Ministries. "Media Update" provides a critical look at secular music and includes media news and reviews of contemporary Christian music.

Contact Menconi Ministries, Box 969, Cardiff, CA 92007 for more information.

More resources are available from interl'inc., a company specializing in resources that combine contemporary Christian music with youth ministry programming. Contact interl'inc., Box 21806, Waco, TX 76702.

Table Talk—Use the "Table Talk" handout (p. 25) as the basis for a parents and kids' meeting. Distribute the handout before the meeting. Open the meeting with fun crowdbreakers and include a time of affirmation for both parents and kids. For crowdbreaker ideas, check out *Quick Crowdbreakers and Games for Youth Groups* (Group Books). Have parents and kids bring favorite records. Then have them rate the songs and discuss the messages in them using the handout as a guide.

LISTEN-TO-THE-MUSIC WORD SEARCH ANSWER KEY

Listen-to-the-Music Word Search—Copy the "Listen-to-the-Music Word Search" (p. 44). Challenge kids to find the hidden words. Have a contest to see who can find them first. Award a cassette of a popular Christian artist as a prize.

Music Evaluation File—Make copies of the "Music Evaluation Form" (p. 45) and give them to your students. Encourage kids to complete the forms for songs they listen to—both Christian and secular. Keep completed forms on file at church for reference. Use them to find songs that might prompt good discussion in other Sunday school activities.

Mega Music Party—Have students bring their favorite records and tapes to a music-listening party. Serve lots of refreshments and play a few games. Tape newsprint to the walls and have kids rate each song from one to 100. Give a prize to the person who brought the tape with the top song. Talk about the messages in the songs.

Talent Show—Invite musical junior highers and middle schoolers in your church to prepare songs for a fun night of music and games. Invite the whole congregation to participate too. Make it a time of fun—not a contest. Award prizes to anyone brave enough to sing in front of the group.

Rockin' Weekend—Plan a retreat based on rock music and the rock of our faith—Jesus. Collect a variety of tapes and records to play during the retreat—both secular and Christian. Have musical members bring guitars and portable keyboards. Also collect a bunch of percussion instruments—wood blocks, triangles.

Some activities you could include: have kids rate songs' music and messages; have a lip-sync contest; sing familiar choruses; have kids write and perform songs; discuss how rock music makes kids feel; compare Christian music with secular music; discuss how Jesus is the rock of our faith; play games such as Musical Chairs, Name That Tune and Music Trivia. Be sure to have lots of food.

PARTY PLEASERS

RETREAT IDEA

LISTEN TO THE MUSIC wordsearch

See how many of the following Christian artists and music-related words you can find. Words may be vertical, horizontal or diagonal.

ALLIES
AMY GRANT
BALLAD
BEAT
BLUES
CONCERT
DANCE
DRUMS
GUITAR
INSTRUMENTS
JAZZ

KIM BOYCE
KIM HILL
LOUD
LYRICS
METAL
MICHAEL PEACE
MICHAEL W SMITH
MUSIC
NEW AGE
PETRA

PUNK
RAP
RICK CUA
ROCK
RUSS TAFF
SONG
STRYPER
SYNTHESIZER
TOUR
VOCALS

```
S W N S E C N A D H G E W R
A F F A T S S U R T T A E B
U T N A R G Y M A I Y Z N B
C R D R U M S G O M I Z B E
K S T N E M U R T S N I A C
C E R J E I R T E W P L L A
I R A T T K L H I L K Y L E
R Z A A B E T L C E I R A P
Z L R Z P N R O I A H I D L
E S T R Y P E R Z H P C S E
A C U S L A C O V C M S W A
R O Y O Z N N C Y I C I O H
T N U O E N O C I M K V K C
E D V W B K C R K N V N Y I
P L A P C M V L G C I S U M
D G N O S O I M B L U E S P
E X R G G R A K S E I L L A
```

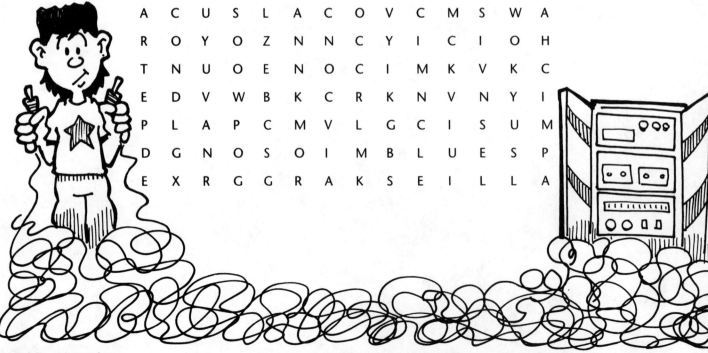

Use this form to evaluate music. Talk about your findings with friends.

Song Title _____

Group or Artist _____

Style of music: (Check those that apply.)
- ☐ rap
- ☐ soul
- ☐ heavy metal
- ☐ jazz

- ☐ rock 'n' roll
- ☐ new age
- ☐ pop
- ☐ Latin

- ☐ reggae
- ☐ punk
- ☐ new wave
- ☐ _____

How good is the music?
☐ Fantastic   ☐ Good   ☐ Okay   ☐ Fair   ☐ Awful

How good is the singing?
☐ Fantastic   ☐ Good   ☐ Okay   ☐ Fair   ☐ Awful

What is the song's message? _____
_____
_____

Is the message compatible with your Christian beliefs?
☐ Yes   ☐ No (explain): _____

What kind of message does the song have?
- ☐ Positive
- ☐ Negative

- ☐ Uplifting
- ☐ Depressing

- ☐ Challenging
- ☐ Entertaining only

Rate the message:
☐ very meaningful   ☐ too basic/simplistic   ☐ too confusing

Comments _____
_____
_____

Overall Rating
☐ Fantastic   ☐ Good   ☐ Okay   ☐ Fair   ☐ Awful

Reviewer _____

Date reviewed _____

More from Group's Active Bible Curriculum

Yes, I want scripture-based learning that blasts away boredom.

For Senior High

Quantity

_____ 202-1 **Getting Along With Parents**
Help senior highers build quality relationships with their parents
ISBN 1-55945-202-1 $6.95

_____ 200-5 **Hazardous to Your Health**
Train senior high students to understand and avoid abusive lifestyles
ISBN 1-55945-200-5 $6.95

_____ 203-X **Is Marriage In Your Future?**
Help teenagers learn what they need to know now—so they can have a successful marriage and family life later
ISBN 1-55945-203-X $6.95

_____ 205-6 **Knowing God's Will**
Help teenagers discover God's will for their lives
ISBN 1-55945-205-6 $6.95

_____ 201-3 **School Struggles**
Train teenagers to turn school stress into school success
ISBN 1-55945-201-3 $6.95

_____ 204-8 **Your Life as a Disciple**
Help Christian teenagers develop a desire to serve God
ISBN 1-55945-204-8 $6.95

For Junior High/Middle School

Quantity

_____ 100-9 **Boosting Self-Esteem**
Help kids develop a positive self-image
ISBN 1-55945-100-9 $6.95

_____ 102-5 **Evil and the Occult**
Train junior highers to protect themselves against the trap of Satanism
ISBN 1-55945-102-5 $6.95

_____ 103-3 **Peer Pressure**
Teach students to make good decisions while keeping their friends
ISBN 1-55945-103-3 $6.95

_____ 104-1 **Prayer**
Help young people discover God through prayer
ISBN 1-55945-104-1 $6.95

_____ 101-7 **Today's Music: Good or Bad?**
Help teenagers make good decisions about music
ISBN 1-55945-101-7 $6.95

_____ 105-X **What's A Christian?**
Teach Christian teenagers the basics of their faith
ISBN 1-55945-105-X $6.95

Yes, please send me _____ of Group's Active Bible Curriculum™ studies at $6.95 each plus $3 postage and handling per order. Colorado residents add 3% sales tax.

03151

▸ ☐ Check enclosed   ☐ VISA   ☐ MasterCard
Credit card # _____
Good until _____

(Please print)
Name _____
Address _____
City _____ State _____ ZIP _____
Daytime phone (___) _____

Take this order form or a photocopy to your favorite Christian bookstore. Or mail to:

Group Books Active Bible Curriculum
Box 481 ● Loveland, CO 80539 ● (303) 669-3836

Blast away boredom with these upcoming scripture-based topics.

For Senior High

- Sexuality
- Making Decisions
- Materialism
- Dangers Around Us: New Age and Cults
- Being a Servant
- Injustice
- Belief-Studies in John
- Resurrection
- Faith in Tough Times

For Junior High

- Temptation: Drugs and Alcohol
- Independence
- Body-Health
- Communicating With Parents
- Relationships: Guys and Girls
- Sharing Your Faith
- Anger
- Creation
- The Bible

For more details write:

Group's Active Bible Curriculum
Box 481 ● Loveland, CO 80539 ● 800-747-6060